With the Faith

of a

Mustard Seed

Tracy McFadden

PublishAmerica
Baltimore

ISBN: 1-4241-9993-X
PUBLISHED BY PUBLISHAMERICA, LLLP
www.publishamerica.com
Baltimore

Printed in the United States of America

This book is dedicated to all those whether voluntarily or involuntarily, who were intricate parts of my journey and to all of those who, through the inspiration of this book, will begin a new journey of their own.

Ephesians 2: 10

"For we are God's workmanship, created in Christ Jesus to do good works, which God prepared in advance for us to do."

With the Faith

of a

Mustard Seed

Chapter One

God has a plan for our lives that is destined to be played out if we open our hearts and souls to him. Can you truly fulfill your destiny when you have wandered far off the path and into darkness that you never want to experience again? I pondered the possibility and with the faith of a mustard seed believed I could be changed. I knew that God was with me even though I was not with him. I got down on my knees and cried out "God, I know you are here with me now; take my hand pull me out of this pit and set my feet back on the right path."

Imagine being raised in a family that was by appearance so perfect that they were lovingly referred to as the "Huckstables". For those of you brought up watching The

Simpsons, the Huckstables was a made for TV family that was virtually perfect. They had all the social graces, no fights or major morality breakdowns, just good old wholesome family charm. I can see why on the surface we seemed the Huckstable family type. We were a close knit family that spent a lot of quality time together. We attended church every Sunday and were active in many aspects of the church. Our parents were the ideal couple, both having strong thriving careers and well known and respected in the community. My dad was an Elder in the church and active in many civic organizations focused on helping others in the community. My brother and I were "fairly" well behaved children; well rounded and on track to follow in our parents footsteps of success. All of our friends loved to hang out at our home. It was as if it was an enticing drug luring them into a world that they only fantasized about having. I was such a lucky girl to be blessed by such a loving and nurturing family that taught me the values of life and set me up for success.

My teen years were relatively uneventful. In fact by most standards they were down right boring. I was very tenacious and not afraid to stand my ground when I believed in something. That in itself was not bad however my heart for the underdog often got me in over my head and certainly did not help me make friends and influence people. While most of the girls in my class were striving to be popular and seeking out the hottest guy in class, I was befriending those who had no friends. As noble as that may sound now at the time it made for a lonely existence. I was in the most peculiar of circumstance in what seemed to be a no win situation. On one hand I had a small group of people putting me on a pedestal as a friend like no other. That someone like me would be seen in the halls with the likes of them was beyond them. Oh, but how far and hard the fall off that pedestal from the hurling of harsh words from the rest of the students. "Little Miss Goody Two Shoes" and "You're a nobody that hangs with the nobody's" they would say. So I just blended in, not totally alone, but definitely ostersized. In fact, at my high school reunion the phrase of the evening would be "Tracy who?"

I graduated in 1984 and married Bryan in December of 1986. Sorry, but little Miss Goody Two Shoes from the Huckstable family has no romantic knight in shining armor story to tell leading up to this marriage. More a Tracy typical boy meet girl story.

Bryan was in the Army at home on recruiter duty when we met so our relationship was a long distance one. The majority of our getting to know one another was via BellSouth.

The proposal was made on the way home from the airport on a short visit home for Bryan. The wedding was planned while the groom was away and would arrive just in time to say "I do". Don't fret; the wedding ceremony was definitely fit for the fairy tale books. We were married in the church that generations of my family had attended. My favorite Youth Minister performed the ceremony. I was in a Snow White gown with a long train and the church was filled with red flowers, Bryan's favorite color, and very fitting for the month of December that it was. My very talented brother sang "There is Love" and "Love me Tender". As we exchanged our vows the minister quoted Ruth: 1: 16 & 17, "Where you go I will go, where you stay I will stay. Your people will be my people and your God my God. Where you die I will die and there I will be buried. May the Lord deal with me, be it ever so severely, if anything but death separates you and me." Now, if you did not feel joined for eternity after this ceremony then there was no chance you ever would!

Life is so ironic. I had come to realize that everything I boldly stated I would not do ended up being the exact thing

I did. It should have been no surprise to my parents when I informed them that my husband had decided to reenlist in the military and I was moving to Missouri; the place I had gone for my senior trip and sworn I would NEVER return to. Oh, but this would be only one of many times I would put my foot into my mouth.

As we packed up the moving van in preparation for the big move I could hardly believe that I was going to leave home. Not only leave "home" but leave the small town in Florida I was born and raised in to venture off to be a new wife in a new state not with palm trees and beaches, but cold winters filled with snow. What a huge turn of events in my life this would inspire. All I could do was pray that my life experience to this point would sustain me to adjust to this enormous change.

We settled into our military living quarters in what became know as "Ft. Lost in the Woods Misery!" The town was dead and so were all the plants due to the unbearably cold weather. There is always a silver lining in every cloud and mine was that I got to see snow for the first time in my life at the age of 20. Bryan however, who was not a native Floridian, was not amused when I woke him up at 5:00 A.M to inform him that it was snowing outside and I wanted to go out and play.

Homesick does not begin to explain what I was feeling being so far away from home. I also desperately missed being in church on Sunday and in search of a Christian Church I went. I settled for a small quaint church in the next town over. Bryan did not share my enthusiasm for attending church so I went alone for the fist few months. The precious memory of the Sunday as I sat in the third to last pew as always and turned around to find my husband standing in the entryway will forever be embedded in my mind. My prayers were answered; he was there. The advice the pastor had given me to not nag but just live by example was excellent advice. We not only became a church going couple but Bryan was baptized in this church. We also participated in a mission to bring the church closer to the base. Every Sunday night we went to the daycare facility we now used on Sunday mornings to hold our service and moved all the toys and cribs and put up folding chairs. I was truly beginning to settle in and make new friends.

Being the naïve young new wife far away from home, I did not realize that being nauseas every morning was not a typical symptom of being homesick. It was more a symptom of being pregnant! Oh yes, to add to the excitement of this portion of my journey I found out I was pregnant. Excitement, fear, excitement, fears.... The emotional roller coaster I was on was a wild ride. Once I was able to truly grasp the fact that I was indeed going to be a mother I was full of nothing but pure joy. By the way, just for reference, I was caught on video tape at my wedding saying I was NEVER going to have children. Now how ridiculous was that. Of course I was going to have children and lots of them.

As I sat talking and singing to this little life inside me I prayed and hoped for a little girl. I could envision all the little dresses, hair pins, dress shoes…it would be so much fun! Then the big day arrived and after twelve long hours of back labor my gorgeous baby girl was born. Words cannot express the love I felt at the moment she was laid in my arms! Nothing on earth can compare to giving birth to a child and nothing on earth could come between her and I.

Time moved on and Brandi began to grow up and needed to have a little brother or sister, preferably a brother to share her life with. Once again I was going to be a mommy. This pregnancy was complicated by the fact that Bryan was very close to getting out of the service. My due date was only a month away from his estimated date of departure and as that date grew closer I moved back home with mom and dad to finish out my term. My prayers were that Bryan would make it home in time for the birth and that this baby would not be late! My prayers were answered in every aspect. Bryan drove all day long to literally come home and find me pacing and saying "dear, I think we need to go to the hospital". Nothing like timing right? But this was only the beginning of sleepless nights to come.

Everything went as planned and my son was born. Once again I felt that overflowing love that is stronger than anything I can compare it to. This time I had a strong and handsome young man who had literally kicked his way into this world. It should be no surprise that he has turned out to be an amazing soccer player.

My husband and I found ourselves settling in once again back in my home town. It was exactly where we were suppose to be, as the home I had grown up in as a young child was run down, in great need of repair and for sale. My parents were willing to co-sign the mortgage and we were able to purchase this property and begin the long, hard path to reconstruct the home in our spare time.

Our marriage had begun with a lot of strain. Moving to a new place, adjusting to a new life and in less than a year of marriage expecting our first child was something that required considerable strength and work. We were a couple who had married as a result of a long distance relationship and were truly getting to know each other in person. Now we were trying to adjust to two children, two jobs and desperately needing to finish the remodeling of our new home. The stress, along with the baggage that we each brought into our marriage, became more than we could handle. After four years and only a few months of being in our new home our marriage was over.

It is amazing how quickly the foundation on which your life was built can crack. "My marriage can't be over" I thought. That went against everything I was raised to believe. Divorce was not an option. Had I not heard the minister's final words: "May the Lord deal with me, be it ever so severely, if anything but death separates you and me". Thus the opening of my pit was dug and the long spiral spin downward was about to begin.

Don't pity me, this divorce was initiated and forced by yours truly. Initially Bryan's defense response was "fine, I do not need you in my life anyway", but he quickly swallowed his pride and tried to find another way around the mess we had made. I however, was having no part of it. My tenacious attributes were in full force at this point and I believed that this marriage was not savable. Satan had dug his claws in deep and continued to whisper in my ear, "don't give up, you are right…you are always right…stand your ground". So out went Bryan and in came total chaos. What Satan tried to convince me was power and control was slowly destroying my life.

I felt like I was in Alice's Wonderland as I tried to find my footing in life. A single mom with lots of responsibility and little stability of mind was a dangerous combination. Top that off with the fact I had led a relatively straight and narrow life in my younger days and Satan had a large playing field to work with. Family and friends with the best of intentions were encouraging me not to dwell on my situation but to start finding new friends and get onto the dating scene. "Why not?" I would say to them. I was on the way to freedom; here was my second chance to live. Every other weekend was a blank canvas for me to spread my wings, as the kids would be with their dad. There was nothing to hold me back and after one push to compromise lead to another, I became a regular member of the bar-hopping party scene. I was like a kid in a candy store and was getting attention I had never experienced before. Keep in mind I was not the most popular girl in high school and now had men who were interested in me like never before.

After sowing a few wild oats an old acquaintance came

into the picture. In my current state of confusion I was extremely susceptible to many traps but little did I know that the snare Satan had set this time was going to clamp down hard and have a lasting impact on this new party girl.

Prince charming had nothing on this guy. Let me paint the picture for you. A mother of two in the process of divorcing and working a full time job while trying to maintain her home is courted by a super hero on his white horse (or pick up truck to be more realistic). I would come home from work yard work is done, the kids toys are fixed and a handsome man is standing in the midst of it all. What girls' heart would not melt? I did not ask for any of this, but he chose to come to my home while I was at work and brighten my day by taking a few chores off my endless weekend list. "Want to go out Friday night?" he would ask. "Are you kidding", I would say? How could I say no after all that he had done? Oh boy, it gets better. This handsome man comes to the door with flowers for the lady and candy for the kids. Let the romance begin; this one seems like a keeper.

Once I was completely overcome by what a great guy this was and how much I needed someone like this in my life, the push came for a "live in" relationship. Wow, now this goes completely against the moral grounds on which I was raised. There was not confusion, however, in the fact that this action would not be God ordained. Should we truly be expected to meet the standards of total perfection? I was already in the "world" so why not continue to justify my downward spiral? The physical, emotional and spiritual weakness I was experiencing at that point left options open for many things that I would have never considered in the past. We moved in together while my divorce was being finalized and eventually decided we should tie the knot. There was no fairy tale wedding this time, rather an outdoor country setting with my two children standing up with me.

In less than six months I came home to a Dear Jane note on the table stating it was over. My knight in shining armor was gone. It was happening all over again. I was getting a divorce and screwing up my life. The laughter from Hell resounded, "Sucker! I got another one!"

Around and around in a downward motion I continued to go. This kick had really hurt and the bitterness and resentment I felt consumed my very soul. Alcohol was the best way to numb the pain and would replace it with temporary satisfaction. I needed help. How could I get out of this mess that I knew was wrong for me? Church was always there throughout this entire mess; something I attended faithfully but I was beginning to realize that showing up and sitting in the pew was not enough for me.

Two years had passed since the beginning of the end of my marriage to Bryan. After a long court battle our marriage had ended and I had re-married and divorced again. But through good and bad Bryan had always been a constant in my life and amazingly even when he was angry with me he never completely shut me out. He always held that glimpse of hope that things could change and we could get back together. I had slapped him in the face pretty hard but his love was as bonding as the vows that were spoken on December 13, 1986.

You guessed it, after my second divorce and an attempt to try and listen to God's direction, I finally decided that maybe Bryan and I could make this work and we began our courtship all over. Dating, along with counseling, made it evident that we wanted to put "us" back together and we were remarried in June 1993.

Common sense would lead you to believe that we had learned a hard lesson and that our marriage would be stronger and more resilient than ever. But the claws of the Devil were still deeply embedded in me and the temptations he had lured me with thus far had enticed me to want more. I was still alive; I was still having fun and there was no harm in continuing to enjoy the life I had been blessed with. During our separation both of us had turned to drinking and partying to cope with the situation and even after we re-married that aspect of our lives was still going strong. The fact we were remarried and had two young children to consider did not seem to faze either of us and we spent many weekends getting a sitter and hitting the town. The alcohol and the party atmosphere lured us into further temptation and we found ourselves making friends with other party types. This dangerous combination pulled me even further into the deep dark pit of despair as we ventured together into the "sex, drugs, and rock and roll" scene and I was on the verge of ending my marriage once again.

The more attention and flattery I received the more I wanted and this experience was filling a void in my life in the most horrendous way. The implications of what I was participating in were mind boggling. The best analogy I can give is Russian roulette, not only for me but for the family that I would die for. What was I doing? Was I willing to sacrifice everything for my own self gratification? I had gone from one extreme to the other. From someone who would sacrifice self-ratification for others to someone that, like a girl lost in the desert, had found water and could not get enough to drink.

It was the words from the mouth of a total stranger that jolted me to reality and pierced my very soul. "You have the love of Jesus in your eyes" they remarked in passing. Where did this random remark come from? Why had this person I had never met before feel the need to make such a peculiar statement? At that very moment the shame I felt was unbearable and I knew without a doubt that my only hope was getting back to God. It was the only chance I had at redemption and putting my life back on track before I destroyed so many peoples lives! The constant guilt of my lying, sneaking and cheating had worn me out completely. I could not allow this charade to continue.

Christ welcomed me back with open arms; the prodigal daughter who had squandered all the gifts that God had given her. I had tried to run the course of my life on my own and failed miserably. Then I came crawling back home with tears in my eyes begging for a second chance that was so not deserved. The mercy of God is such an amazing thing! I thank God we do not have to earn mercy by our works but receive it by just turning to him and asking.

When I turned my eyes to Jesus I knew that I needed to have an intimate relationship with him to stay out of the pit I had fallen into. I needed to establish a new pattern of speaking to God on a daily basis. One theory says that you form a habit by doing the same thing for 21 consecutive days. My first step was to start a morning devotion time to test this theory. I began every day reading His word and speaking with Him if only for a few minutes. A monumental change began to take place in my life. God was unraveling my life's purpose day by day in some of the most subtle ways.

I want to share with you my experience over the last six years. God has now given me insight into my journey and the role his direction has played in placing me exactly where I am today. I believe with all my heart and soul I am exactly where God predestined me to be.

Chapter Two

Being the personality type that must have complete control in all aspects of my life, I scheduled my devotion time for 5:30 AM before the rest of the family was awake and my day began. I went to the Christian book store to purchase a women's devotional book to help me get started. As the days turned into months I began to notice the words were speaking directly to me. How could this randomly chosen devotional book know exactly what I needed to hear at this point in my life? Could this be the voice of God I had always hoped to hear? Did I truly want to hear it? What kind of responsibility would that put on me? I could no longer hide behind the excuse of not knowing what God wanted me to do. It was becoming abundantly clear.

I had just started a new position as an Administrative Assistant to an eccentric entrepreneur/engineer. I had known Norman for years through my previous employment with the county. The warnings came from every direction. "You're going to work for Norman?" some would comment. "He cannot keep an assistant for more than six months!" He did not have the reputation of being the best boss but I thrive from a challenge and decided my goal would be to make it six months and one day; then no matter what happened at that point I would be the winner!

Things from my perspective were going great. It was month three and I had made it half way through my goal. No major issues had arisen. The quirks of his personality were manageable and I was feeling pretty confident that I may be the world champ of this competition. Then late one afternoon Norman called me into his office with a rather serious look on his face. As I sat in my "assistant's" chair next to his desk he said "I don't think you are cut out for this job, you are way to humble. It must be that Christianity thing". Let me set the stage for the personality type I was dealing with. Picture someone who is very intelligent, has lots of money, and is able to use his money and power to get whatever he wants. He expected the use of this power to be exerted by anyone working directly for him, especially his assistant. His remarks, intended to be critical, were the greatest compliment I had ever received! He thought I was humble? What had I done to suggest that? At that moment God enlightened me to the fact that if Christ is truly living in us he shines through in our everyday lives. Flustered because he did not anticipate the reaction he got from me, he gathered his things to leave. "Do I come back to work tomorrow?" I thought. "Was this just a warning of unhappiness?" I just had to make it to six months and one day so back to work I came the next day.

Not wanting to fire me, he decided to send me to manage another aspect of his business ventures. Of course it was an area I had no expertise or knowledge in and it was delivered with a sink or swim undertone. "Your position here will no longer be available" Norman stated with confidence. He was moving me over to help manage a manufactured home community he owned. I was starting to lean on Christ for strength and direction. If He wanted me to stay at this job then I am sure He would help me survive this transition.

Help me survive He did. After my first year I was really starting to get the hang of things. Not by coincidence, some of the sub-contractors we were using were fellow Christians who, instead of getting amusement out of watching the "chick" screw up, stepped up to the plate and helped me adapt, learn and survive. As time past I continued to grow successful and ultimately became the manager of every aspect of the community. I was learning from real life experience how to handle sales, marketing, construction and HOA management. What seemed a virtually impossible task to be taken on by a St.Cloud High School graduate had turned into a very successful venture with the profability of this arm of his ventures increasing significantly. Amazing what God can do with the seemingly uneducated and weak. Through him they can become very strong!

God, through his generosity, gave me many opportunities to touch the lives of families in the community where I was working. Several residents began attending church. I was able to make an impression on other residents as well with my Christ like attitude in life. I was told by the president of the Homeowner's Association in the community that I would never be a success in life because I was too nice. I guess that depends on your definition of success.

The one thing I loved most about my job was being a part of so many wonderful people's lives. They truly blessed my life. God used this time in my life to take me out of my comfort zone and put me in the perfect position to learn people skills. He showed me how to share the love he gave me with others and let me see what a rejuvenating experience it could be. He brought Mr. Stokes into my life who, despite his unpopularity within the community, became a close friend not only to me but to my family. We adopted him as a surrogate dad/grandpa and established a life long bond.

My relationship with Norman had taken a lot of twist and turns over this time period. Originally he sent me out to fall flat on my face but when I landed on my feet it got his attention. We began to get back on good terms and my office became a place of refuge for him at times. When he needed to vent or just catch his breath from the whirlwind of his life, he would come to sit and chat. These visits were usually very early in the morning as I was usually in the office by 7:00 AM. Over time the conversations began to wander away from work and into personal philosophy. I was so intrigued with his analogies of life and truly enjoyed the exchange of ideas we would share. I found it interesting that he would at times ask questions about my faith and my relationship with Christ; trying to figure out from an analytical point of view the rational of this giving up of control to an unseen force.

As time progressed I would even get a few questions like "What would be the Christian thing to do in this situation?" It was as if God was speaking to his heart through our relationship, no matter how strained it was at times. Our differences were our enemy and our friend the relationship walked that fine line of love and hate.

That line was a very dangerous one to be walking. It was like a tight rope that I was subject to fall off of at any moment and the fall would be long and hard. My mind flashed back to the pit from which I had recently crawled out of and I was able to see the danger of stepping back into Satan's trickery. "Oh God, please guide my path keep my feet on the right path" was my prayer. I never forgot that my sinful nature could win if I did not stay focused daily on the One who can overcome.

Business was booming and I was feeling very confident in my accomplishments. This "chick" had come and conquered, but the fire was still within me to accomplish more and do better every day. My new found confidence gave me more stamina to stand up to Norman and defend my business decisions. When I called him to tell him I had fired one of his "buddy" contractors because they had stood me up on the job for the last time, he was speechless. Norman speechless? Never! He backed me up, though, as I had a very valid reason for my actions. I will never forget the next morning when I arrived at 7:00 AM to find Norman sitting in the clubhouse with the stereo playing "Every Rose Has It Thorns", drinking his cup of coffee and saying with a smile on his face "let's chat".

Things were really starting to become confusing in my mind. This person that had so many attributes I despised was becoming enticing in other ways. It was as if he had dual personalities. On one hand he could be so callous and self centered yet on the other so caring and giving. Oh, the many faces of deception and entrapment.

We both had very analytical minds and I was so energized by our conversations. Anticipation of our times together became increasingly more frequent as I had no other person with whom I could have such stimulating conversations. Red flags started to go up in my head. This relationship was becoming dangerously close to an inappropriate one and I had to pray daily for strength and wisdom to continue this relationship while not being tripped up by Satan's subtle attempt to have me return to my sinful nature.

Chapter Three

After about two years of this spiritually strengthening exercise God was ready to move me forward to my next area of service. I developed an overwhelming urge to become a mother again. Being unable to have any more children of my own, I was drawn to the possibility of adoption. The further I explored my feelings and determining whether or not they were sent by God the more I realized I needed to help a child that was less fortunate. God had so richly blessed me and my family's lives. What better way to repay the debt than to adopt an elementary school age child? After approaching my husband and then the rest of our family with what I felt God was calling us to do, we prayerfully moved forward. We began taking the necessary steps to become adoptive parents. We just knew this would be a quick process. We didn't want a small precious baby; we were willing to take a six to ten year old child that needed a home. There had to be so many possibilities there for us to choose from. I soon learned that it was God's plan, not mine, that was going to be fulfilled.

After a year of attempting to adopt a child with no success I began to question my calling to this mission. On our annual family weekend trip to the beach I sat on the shoreline and cried out to God "What is it that you want me to do? Why have you brought me here and slammed so many doors in my face?" My heart ached because I truly wanted to do God's will for my life. I just needed him to be clearer on exactly what that was. You know the saying "be careful what you ask for?" Well let me tell you, in that moment God granted my request and replied with an answer I was not expecting. As the rays from the sun beamed down it was as if heaven was opening just for me. God spoke to me not in an audible voice, but thru my very soul. He told me to do the one thing I always said I could not and would not do.

He wanted me to be a foster parent first. "Come on God, you know who you are talking to here" I said. "I cannot take in a child, love them, nurture them and then let them go." No matter how many excuses and reasons I conjured up as to why this was not the right choice, God did not change his mind. He simply replied that I could not do it alone but through him (Philippians 4:13 "I can do everything through him who gives me strength".)

This became my first real leap of faith. God said "If you believe in me then become a foster parent." I walked back up the beach to the hotel where we were staying; the entire time wondering how to explain this one to my husband. My burning desire to be a mother was bad enough since our children were teenagers and close to leaving the nest. Now I was telling him that I wanted to do the one thing I said I would never do and he was coming along for the ride!

I walked into the room and changed my clothes, as we were preparing to go out to dinner. Throughout the entire evening I rehearsed in my mind how I would explain God's direction to Bryan. We were both faithful Christians however my story of God speaking to me from the summer sky was probably going to initially make my husband think his wife had been out in the sun a little too long. We returned from dinner and the kids settled into their side of the room to watch TV and Bryan and I went out on the balcony to enjoy the evening sunset. This was the perfect time to share my experience. Surely the magic of the beauty of the ocean view and darkening sky would make my experience more real to him than a side effect of over exposure to the sun. I took a deep breath and began to tell him of the direction I received from God himself. I was expecting a reaction of "Are you crazy?" We have had this discussion before and this was not the way it ended. But my accommodating husband said "If this is what God wants us to do then that is what we are going to do."

When we returned home we researched what needed to happen to make it possible to become foster parents and we took the additional steps required to obtain our foster license.

After a year and a half of waiting with no child in our home we were extremely anxious to become foster parents. It seems human nature always lets sin creep back into our lives in one form or another. One of my biggest weaknesses is my inability to be still and let God have control. It is the "be still" part that is so challenging to me. When I set my mind on a mission there is nothing or no one that is going to stop me. At least that's what I thought until God showed me otherwise.

I wanted to have a child now! We had been waiting for over a year and were ready to get things going. I had seemed to forget who was steering and had been guiding this ship on its voyage all along. I decided I was smart enough to take the wheel.

We received a phone call that there was a six year old girl in need of a foster home. We immediately jumped in the car and went to the facility she was staying at to meet her. We visited with her and spoke with the care givers at the facility. As we got in the car to leave she was on the playground swinging. She gave us that look that melts your heart and the family pleaded with me to take her home. We called the caseworker and asked what needed to take place for that to happen. Surprisingly we were able to take her right then and there. My inner voice was saying "Wait, you are moving too fast. Things are not as they appear here.... Wait!" But my family's pleading swayed me and I convinced myself the nagging feelings were only nerves. So we brought home our first foster child; a six year old girl. We had the most sincere intentions and gave all our energy to making it work. But God was not the designer of this plan. His energy was not being poured into us and we began to hit many walls that would block us from the assistance we needed. We were in a situation we were not equipped to handle. Our first experience as foster parents ended with her being moved to a therapeutic home that could better deal with all her issues. The lesson learned at this point for me was that when you take the wheel and don't have the directions, you are bound to get lost.

My not following God's direction, be it with good intentions, not only affected my family but this precious child who now had one more negative event in her life.

God does not always take away the consequences of our disobedience but He will always stand beside us during the storm. He never left my side in spite of my actions. He helped me back on my feet to continue the journey he had planned for me all along.

My guilt was not the only repercussions of my bad decision. The agency now doubted our ability to be foster parents and we were given a break to get our thoughts together. The statement was even made that I was not cut out to be a foster mom. Oh, how true that statement was but as God had told me on that shoreline months before with him "nothing is impossible." In fact he would take the impossible and make it possible.

Chapter Four

I may have stumbled a little at the beginning of my journey but I was determined to get back on my feet and continue with God's plan. Little did I know that our lives were about to be turned upside down. A phone call came for the placement of an 18 month old girl who was returning to her mother in about three weeks. I had learned my lesson the first time and I asked God if we should move forward with this. It could be an opportunity to test how we would handle a younger child and break us back into the foster parent world slowly since it was only a three week venture. I had been blessed with being able to move forward and she came into our lives.

We will never begin to understand what God has in

store for us, what lessons he has to teach or what blessings he needs us to give. We can only trust and obey.

I still remember her arrival at our home. As she walked up the sidewalk I ran out to greet her; the sad little face with such a lost look in her eyes. She immediately reached for me to pick her up as if she saw the love of Jesus in my eyes. We quickly discovered that she suffered from a disease that was contagious and would require multiple surgeries. My initial response was concern for my family. I decided that I would be the only diaper changer and would always wear gloves. With research I became very knowledgeable of the symptoms and in the ways it could be contracted. Knowledge and common sense can go a long way and God gave me the inner peace to know that He would not allow any harm to come to my family. So we took that leap of faith again and moved forward with God. I spent many days and nights loving this child through a very rough time in her life. We had been through so much together and I felt as if she was my child. The connection was apparent to others, many of whom thought she was my child and commented on how much we looked alike. I beamed with pride every time. Due to our discovery she was not returned to her mom in three weeks. Contrary to the original plan, our journey with her continued for a year and a half.

The job God had so strategically placed me in a couple of years before gave me the ability to be flexible with my time and work from home when necessary. This was crucial during the times she had surgery and needed time to heal before returning to daycare. Norman, despite his generosity of time off, was not sure my decision was the smartest. Our philosophical talks turned to analyzing the pros and cons of this mission I had taken and he adamantly tried to convince me that I needed to get out of this situation. As time went on I began to see signs of jealousy from Norman. He was angry that this child was taking so much of my attention, time and energy. I am not sure why that was a bone of contention with him as my work was not showing signs of distress. I was available by phone or e-mail 24/7 and was coming in the evenings or on weekends to meet with potential buyers and handle any on-site issues that needed my attention.

Norman's demands for all my attention was starting to strain our relationship once again. I knew that he thrived on finding my breaking point and I was being pushed to the brink at times. The stress of trying to balance everything began to take its toll on me. Upon returning to my normal work schedule I was welcomed back with a list of things gone wrong from Norman, which pushed me over the edge. I was feeling used and unappreciated. Here I had worked from home to keep the business running and his profits pouring in when I could have used some of the six weeks of vacation time I had accumulated, while letting him figure out how to handle things while I was gone. Life definitely would have been easier for me as I could have slept while she was napping, which would have done wonders since we were almost always up all night.

I began to evaluate my situation and where my priorities were. Why was I willing to sacrifice so much of myself and my life for a job when God had given me a much larger and more fulfilling responsibility and purpose in life? Why was this person able to push and push and I just kept coming back for more? I prayed every single morning for direction from God "How can I balance all these things? Show me the direction you desire me to go and bring some peace back into my life."

Once again God was going to test my faith. He asked that I quit the job that had turned from a six month and one day commitment to a four year venture. I had grown so immensely from this leg of my journey. The community and my fellow employees were like family to me. I had been so successful in a venture that could have been a disaster and moving out of this comfort zone was not my first choice. To top it off money had come with my success and I was making a salary that I would never have imagined being a high school graduate with no college background. The sacrifice being asked of me this time was monumental to my perspective of my life. In my calculations, with my education and experience, we were looking at about a $30,000 a year pay cut when I had to find a "real" job. My experiences with Norman were unique in so many ways and had opened up opportunities that were not going to be available in the corporate world. And there were not a lot of "Normans" out there looking for a jack-of-all-trades. Ironically the fears that were running through my mind were the very reasons that I needed to move on. I was becoming dependant on my own abilities for my stability. How easily I had forgotten that it was by the grace of God that I was able to achieve all that had been accomplished. God was the only one to fear and if He said "Time to move on", then I needed to move on and know that He will provide for my needs, but not always my wants.

I could feel Satan warming up for the kill so I picked up the phone and called Bryan to meet me for lunch. If this wasn't done swiftly the opening for Satan would be too large and he would definitely force his way in. Bryan and I decided to go to the lakefront and chat.

Here I once again had to explain to Bryan how God had asked me to make a move that had no apparent logic to it. This move was definitely going to impact the entire family as our budget would become something we had to watch. The luxuries of weekend trips to the beach, eating out whenever we wanted and hitting the sales racks at the mall would now come to a skreetching halt. After about half an hour of discussing the implications of this decision and concluding that we would make lifestyle changes Bryan seemed resolved that it was for the best. Neither of us was fearless but we both knew we had reached a point that something had to change. If God's will was that this was the solution then we would have the faith to follow his direction and trust in his grace and mercy. It was the only reason we had survived to date, so taking control ourselves was not an option.

I typed my resignation letter and prepared myself for the reaction of the boss who thought we would grow old and grey together. Despite his initial disregard for my Christian standards he had taught me so much about myself. Our unique relationship had made me a much stronger person and pushed me to a stronger relationship with God. He was going to be caught totally off guard. I know God always has a reason for the way and times things are done, so I knew in my heart that this was something that would ultimately benefit Norman as well.

I tried to get a moment of Norman's time the next day before our Homeowners meeting that evening. As usual Norman was running like crazy and had pushed me to the bottom of the list, so I was unable to share my news until after our meeting that night. How ironic that on this particular night Norman had come to the Homeowners meeting and actually stood up and praised me for the work I had done despite the enormous challenge it was to work with him. "Oh no" I thought, "there goes Satan with a last ditch effort to play on my guilt and make me rethink leaving this position." No, God was abundantly clear on what he wanted me to do. Not only was Bryan at peace about this but my teenage children, who were going to feel the impact as well, were just thrilled that they would have their mom back for more than an hour or two a week. "Nice try Satan" I thought, "You get an "A" for effort."

The meeting came to an end and as soon as we could break away from the crowd, I told Norman I needed to speak with him. "Tonight?" he asked. "Yes please. This is important and I have been trying to get to you all day" I replied. To have some privacy we sat in my vehicle and I took a deep breath and made my delivery. Once it was out Norman asked "Is this a personal decision? Is it because of me?" I could not find words and stayed silent for a moment. "Where are you going?" he asked. "I am not sure, I just know here is not for me anymore" I replied. "I will help you with anything you need you know that right? I will always be here for you should you ever need me." As these words bounced around the vehicle my mind wandered to the story of Peter stepping out of the boat and walking on the water to Jesus. As long as he kept his eyes focused on Jesus with his arms outstretched to receive, him he would not sink. But the moment he lost that focus he sank. I did not want to sink so during the entire conversation with Norman I envisioned Jesus standing behind him with his hands outstretched to me and I kept moving toward him.

Norman took the news better than I had anticipated. A co-worker later told me that she ask him to give me whatever I wanted so I would stay. The same man who had mocked my Christianity four years prior told her that I was following my Christian heart and he could not compete with that. Wow! Jesus is amazing! Even with my slips and falls he had used me to impact Norman's life and I was not even aware of my influence. How humbling it is to know that God works in our everyday lives to influence the people we come in contact with. He even found a way to use Norman to make a positive impact on my life and we were both stronger better people from the experience.

I gave a months notice and did not pursue any job opportunities during that time. I just finished off my current responsibilities. I recalled the scripture in Colossians 3:23, "Whatever you do work at it with all your heart as if working for the Lord, not for men."

On my final day I packed up my personal belongings and drove away to whatever new adventure God had in store. The Michael W. Smith CD I had been listening to on the way to work popped on and these are the words that were being softly sung while at the time the Spirit let me know they were coming directly from heaven, "May the Lord make his face to shine upon you, give you peace, woo you in, change your heart, make you his forever". I was ready for the next chapter of my journey to begin.

Chapter Five

Now I had some quality time for my family and was able to spend more focused time at home. After a few weeks I began my job search. I sent in a dozen resumes and then came across an ad for an executive assistant to the Vice President of Land Development. With my unique skills I knew this was the perfect job for me. My mom was becoming concerned that I did not yet have a job. My assuring her that God was going to take care of me was not quelling those worries. God made mothers to nurture and be concerned about their children no matter their age! I called to let her know I had found the right job for me and sent in my resume. I was certain a call would come by the end of the week. Sure enough the call came and I went to the interview only to have more confirmation that this was exactly where God wanted me to be. The person who previously held the position had quit on the exact same day I quit my former job. They had been looking for a month for a replacement. I began my new job a week later.

During this time things were beginning to escalate with our foster daughter. She had been having unsupervised weekend visits with her parents. She was coming back saying some very disturbing things that I could not ignore or justify. I relentlessly reported my concerns to anyone who would listen. I was persistent and would not give up. The decision was made to remove her from our home and placed her in temporary care while the situation was fully investigated. Not only did they decide to remove her, but did so at 11:00 at night. Needless to say I had a very restless night as I prayed for some sort of understanding and peace. Why would God allow her to be put through this? Did he not place her in our home for stability and love? My heart was literally breaking into pieces. How in the world was I going to hold together through this? I wanted so desperately to reach out hug her and tell her it was okay. She needed to know we loved her and only wanted the best for her. God had given me an angel here on earth to help me through this journey in her Guardian a Litem. She stayed in contact with her new foster mom and spoke to me daily to ensure me that she was okay and in a loving home. How could I have doubted? There had to be a reason this happened. God had made sure she was put in a safe haven. So I took a deep breath, thanked God for his grace, and moved forward one day at a time. I prayed constantly for the strength to make it through each day. I realized that this situation had produced a positive by-product. My dependence on Jesus had become extremely strong and I was talking to him more deeply and frequently than ever. Then a month later the call I had prayed for came. She could come back to our home. Praise God! "Thank you Jesus!" was my immediate response. Then came the BUT…. A court hearing was scheduled in two weeks and they were recommending reunification with her parents. How quickly my bubble was burst and I felt a huge lump in my throat. I knew I had to see her again and that without a doubt God was giving me the opportunity to end this on a positive note. I had convinced myself that God would make his presence known and she would not go back to her parents. I spoke with my family to get their reaction to seeing her again, knowing she would most likely go back home again in a couple of weeks. Without hesitation the answer was yes. We all had such an incredible bond with her and missed her so! We were reunited on the Fourth of July weekend and were to meet the current foster mom at a gas station on our way to our annual beach visit. My mind was racing and my heart overflowing with joy because I was going to hold her again! So many questions ran through my mind, "Would she be mad at me for allowing her to be taken out of our home or for not talking to her in a month? She is only two; does she have these thoughts? What will the reunion be like?" As she was taken out of the car I heard her precious voice cry out "mommy" as she came to me with outstretched arms. She squeezed my neck so tight that for a moment I stopped breathing. As the air came back into my lungs and the tears ran down my face I thanked God for this moment that I would never forget. The complete love and confidence she seemed to still have in me was overwhelming and humbling. I was floating on Cloud Nine as I took her to our car and prepared her for the drive to the hotel.

We spent the weekend playing on the beach, running from the waves and building sandcastles. As I sat watching her smile, laugh and play I looked up into the same heavens I had several years prior seeking direction. It was not a coincidence that I was in the very same spot in a very different circumstance. This time my cry to the heavens was a pleading for His will, with a large undertone of my own desire to keep her forever. God knew my heart at this moment in time. He knew how much I wanted to have things my way but at the same time truly wanting God's will for her life. So many times Christian well wishers had said they would pray she be kept in our home. Although it was what I so desperately wanted as well, I would tell them we should pray that God's will be done in her life. I had learned that even though I may not understand the "why" of God's direction, it was always for the good and never to bring harm. Jeremiah 29:11 states "For I know the plans I have for you, declares the Lord, plans to prosper you and not to harm you, plans to give you hope and a future." I knew that He would do what was best for her because He promised in His word, and that was all I needed to know. I had to prepare myself to be able to hold this belief should the storm waters begin to rise and the one thing I so dreaded come to pass. I smiled and shed a tear at the same time as the heavens now had the same clarity and beauty as years ago. Heaven's doors were once again open and Jesus was smiling with delight. I was reminded of the direction I had received before and the knowledge that I could do all things through Christ who strengthened me. This time the crashing waves had much more clarity than before.

When I awoke the next morning she climbed up on the

bed and just patted my face as if to make sure she was not dreaming. I chocked back the tears and began to tickle her. I so loved to hear her contagious laugh. The weekend ended all too soon. I wished I had the ability to stop time and stay in that moment forever. I had a feeling that once we went back home our lives would never be the same.

Two weeks later came the day I had dreaded. God woke me at 4:00 AM and let me know she was going home. I went into the bathroom because I was feeling sick. Then I crawled back in bed and bawled. My husband attempted to comfort me as I told him through my sobs that she was going home today. "You don't know for sure" my husband said. I did! And I wasn't sure I could bear the pain. God new I could and gave me this early morning hour to release my pain and prepare myself. I needed to have the strength it was going to take to make this moment in her life as positive as possible. All that was important at that moment was her well being and peace of mind. I will never forget my last moments with her as we packed the car and she prepared to go home. "See you later mommy" she said as the door closed. "How can a two year old understand she will not see me later?" I wondered. The emptiness I felt at that moment was indescribable. It was as if a piece of my very soul was ripped out and taken away, never to return.

This was a day in my life that will forever be in my heart and mind. It was also a huge draw to Jesus that ultimately has brought me so many blessings. My relationship with him became even more intimate. I needed him so completely and desperately and that would open the door for many more blessings yet to be seen.

I was also once again receiving a jolt from my job. We were told that the company was being bought out by another company but, not to worry, our jobs were not in jeopardy.

I really was not worried at this point because I strongly believed that God had brought me to this place for a reason. Then the person through whom I felt God had brought me here was leaving and I became a little insecure in my faith. I began tying to analyze why this was happening. "Am I suppose to be here and if so what does this mean?" I wondered. I prayed about it and at this point felt that God wanted me to be still and do my job. That's exactly what I did.

My passion for my former foster daughter and her situation did not subside. I went through many emotions with God. I fell at his feet and asked "Why are you breaking my heart? Why are you putting that precious child back into an obviously dangerous situation? You are God! You are in control! You can stop this! Why? Why? Why?" I fell to my knees with my hands outstretched like a child who so desperately wanted to be held by her father to feel safe, secure and loved. That wish was granted. I felt at that very moment as if there were arms around me comforting me and letting me know it would be okay. This was the closest I have ever felt to God in my life! I actually felt His presence in the room with me and for a moment I shuttered in fear.

Although I do not pretend to understand why God sent her home I have come to terms with the fact that He is God, He is all knowing, and I am at peace with that. I believe at that moment God let me feel a mustard seed of what He must have felt when He gave His only son for my sins. If he could go through that pain then I could surely go through this heartache with Him. Go with me He did!! He fulfilled my passion to pursue not only my former foster daughter's case but many other children that were probably in the same situation. I was told I could not take on the system. "Who did I think I was?" some would say. "This was David against Goliath and I could not win." Obviously they did not understand the story. Yes, I was in fact like David, with God on my side, and just like David I would be victorious one day over my Goliath. So off I went to speak to the committee that oversees the foster care system. I told my story with apparently a little too much passion and information. My Goliath struck back by putting me on probation for violation of a confidentiality agreement. God was bigger and the committee created an "at large" position, which I was nominated and selected for. God had once again positioned me right where He wanted me to be.

Several months after our last foster daughter was returned we had our next child placed with us; a little girl that was 12 months old. Things were finally starting to turn our way. We were finally being invited to adoption events so we could meet potential children available for adoption. At the first event we were invited to we viewed pictures of children available while pushing our foster daughter in her stroller. There were many displays with photos and write-ups about them and there were caseworkers available to discuss the children with us as well. There she was! A photo of an adorable four year old girl and she was available. Maybe we had a chance. The line was long for her caseworker as she was the youngest child being shown that day. We finally spoke with the caseworker and got a brief description of her situation. She had fetal alcohol syndrome and was developmentally behind. We filled out the required paperwork to put our family in the running to be her permanent family. When we got home my adrenaline was pumping. Here is a little girl God is going to bless me with, my little girl after all!! I got on the internet and started my research into fetal alcohol syndrome and the issues we could be facing in the future if we were the chosen family. I prayed "Please let this be the one. We would love her God you know that. I will learn everything I can about her condition and bring her to her full potential in life." So we prayed and patiently waited to see what would happen. In the meantime we were invited to a second adoption event. This event was at a local sports arena and the children would actually be in attendance. Once again, with foster daughter in tow, we went to the event. I began to feel uneasy as soon as we arrived. We were given specially colored name tags to be designated as potential adoptive parents. Our children were also given special tags to let everyone know they were taken and not children looking for a home. Wow! What an uncomfortable environment to be in; "shopping" for a child much like a pet shop with the child trying to obtain your attention and saying "Pick me, please pick me." If I felt this uncomfortable, imagine how the children must have felt. I looked at my husband and said, "I am not sure I want to stay this is crazy. I feel very uncomfortable here." Then out of the corner of my eye I saw the cutest boy sitting on a bench. I was drawn to this boy in a way I could not explain and could not shake. He was so cute with his baseball cap on sideways. I caught up with the rest of my family as they strolled around the facility. I told them about the boy and to my amazement they had all separately seen him and been drawn to him. "Was this a sign?" I thought. We located a caseworker to find out more about him. I explained that he looked to be about eight. The caseworker was puzzled. "Do you see him anywhere?" she asked. "Please point him out." When we did she said "He is not eight, he is thirteen!" Without any further discussion she ran off to get him to come over and talk with us. We felt a little panic. We did not feel a teenager was something we could handle at this point. My kids piped up, "Mom, do not talk to him. We feel bad. We are not looking to adopt a teenager!" Ready or not here he came, headed straight for us. We had to follow through. The irony of this became clearer as we were introduced. "This is Brian" the caseworker said. It couldn't be simply a coincidence that both my husband and son are named Bryan. He was very shy and hid behind the caseworker. She pushed and prodded for him to talk with us and I became frustrated. "It is okay to be shy, don't worry about it" I said, wanting to put him at ease. This was not a dog and pony show; these were real kids and my love was growing already without a single word being said. We spent the next few hours speaking with Brian and eventually he joined in the conversation. It came time for us to go and we wondered how to say goodbye. It was a very awkward moment. It was apparent he wondered if we were interested and we did not want to give false hope to a boy who had been through more heartbreak than most adults. We told him it was wonderful talking to him and that he was an amazing kid but we needed to head out, as we had a long drive back home. We walked out of the complex and searched for the caseworker. We wanted to know more about Brian. We were feeling a strong pull to him that we could not explain. This was way out of the realm of what we intended when this journey started. We found her and gave her our phone number. We ask that she give us a call when we could come in and look over his files to see if this was something we could handle. I looked up and out of the corner of my eye and saw him looking through the window of the doors to the complex. He had been watching to see if we just left or spoke with the caseworker. He had a smile on his face and

I could not help but to wave and smile as we left. On the way home we talked about our experience and our feelings about Brian. To my surprise my teenage kids were actually very receptive to the idea. My son even said, "I really mean it this time Mom. In the past I just agreed because I knew you wanted it. This time it is a good feeling I have." My daughter, who was getting ready to leave for college, was receptive but in a different phase of her life. She would not be home full time. Maybe the fact that our foster daughter was constantly whining and throwing food had some impact on the decision they were making. Whatever it was I had a good feeling in my soul about this one. Not wanting to do anything rash, we decided to take this slow and do all our homework so we would completely understand what we were getting into. One week later I received the call I had been waiting for. We had been selected to take the four year old little girl. My first reaction was excitement. Finally the little girl I had wanted the past three years. But then I remembered my feeling for Brian and I was very torn. "Why is life so challenging? Why couldn't it just be the girl I wanted?" I wondered. "Why was Brian thrown in the mix just before this call?" I spoke with the caseworker for Brian and set up an appointment to come in and review his files. That same day I was going to review the file for the little girl as well. The appointment was two weeks away and I thought I had plenty of time to convince God that the little girl was the way to go.

Over the next week I spoke to God daily about our decision and which way he wanted us to go. The answer was coming through very clear but I kept resisting because it was not the answer I was hoping for. Then a call cam from the girl's caseworker and they needed to move her sooner than expected. "Would we be able to move forward soon?' they asked. I stalled. With a year old foster child in our home we would need to have her placed in a new home before we could move forward with the adoption. Once again I bought some more time for God to change his mind, but why would I want him to? The vision of Brian sitting on the bench with his sideways cap and his look of desperate need for acceptance and love would forever be imbedded in my mind. Instead of the memory of the first time your baby is laid in your arms, I would have that moment to hold on to as the day I became his mother. Then I remembered the long line of potential parents waiting for the little girl and the fact that we were the only ones in line to take a teenage boy. I was humbled by the Holy Spirit touching my heart and reminding me of the true purpose for which I had started this journey. It was not to stand in the longest line or to fulfill my personal desires. It was to be Christ-like to a child that no one else was willing to reach out to. I called my husband and discussed how he felt about our situation. He had already decided on Brian. So we decided on what we knew was the right thing to do. I called and told the little girl's caseworker to take the next matching family for her as we had decided to move forward with Brian. In that brief phone call I was forever closing the door on my own desires and moving forward with Christ to the place he had been preparing me for. God must have a sense of humor. Why else would he give me a teenage boy and send my only daughter off to college. The next week we went to the office to review the files. Wow! What a life he had experienced! There were stacks of binders full of data on his life and none of it was pretty. In fact some of it was down right intimidating. The other amazing thing about this case was the long history of foster care and abuse this family had. It went back generations. God knew the cycle needed to be broken and a new journey started for this family. He was going to use us to accomplish that. The prospective task seemed incredibly overwhelming. After a couple of hours of reading and skimming through the most recent volumes we decided to take a walk to clear our heads and give our eyes a break. As we walked we had a pure moment of panic. "This may be more than we are able to handle" I said. "This is going to be extremely challenging." Then that little voice in the core of my soul was saying, "You can do all things through me, all things!" We went back and during the next few hours we finished our assessment of Brian's files. We were given the name and number of the current foster parents and were also given the number of the past foster family who had Brian from the beginning. They would be very knowledgeable of his situation. I made some phone calls to each of them and gained more insight into the current status of Brian as well as some past history. We were told that we could not expect any bonding or to be called 'Mom" and "Dad" for some time since he had a current relationship with his biological mother. This was yet another twist in our mission. The judge had felt it best physiologically that Brian be allowed supervised visits with his Mother who had signed her parental rights away. It would be the choice of the adoptive parents as to whether or not that relationship should continue. I was also told by one of the foster parents that because I was not a stay-at-home mom it would not be possible for me to handle this responsibility. Nothing said or put in writing would make me want to turn away. Don't get me wrong, I had my anxiety but I also had a deep inner peace that was bigger than those fears. God said, "I am with you so you cannot fail." There are so many times when we forget the almighty power of God. There is nothing he cannot overcome no matter what the textbooks and therapists say. My God can raise the dead. I had no doubt that he could overcome Brian's challenges and obstacles. So once again we took a leap of faith and called the caseworker. We told her we wanted to adopt Brian to start the visitation process. The first time we visited Brian we met at The Olive Garden for dinner. It was a great time as we ate, talked and became acquainted. The shy little boy we met at the sports arena was showing his true colors and did not stop talking this time. When dinner was complete we had the caseworker take individual pictures of Brian as well as a family picture with all of us together. The smile on his face said it all. I could just see the anticipation in his eyes as he saw there was hope of becoming a part of a real family. "How many days till I can move in?", he asked. "Not until the end of May when school is out. It is only a couple of months away." I replied. "I guess I will just have to wait" he said. We immediately took the pictures and had an 8 x 10 made. Our hallway is the "Hall of Family Photos" and we wanted to have his picture up prior to his first visit. We wanted him to know he was already a part of this family and were just going through the necessary motions to make it official. Our next visit was at a local park where we met for a picnic, played volleyball and took a walk.

We enjoyed each others company and got to know each other a little more. We brought Brian a copy of the pictures we had taken at the prior visit to show to his current foster family and friends. I thought at that moment how God had given me a taste of what it is like on the other side. We had to have supervised visits at first to make sure the match was going to work out. It gave me a glimpse of the feelings of only being able to see your child for a weekend visit. Brian was delighted with the pictures and quickly tucked them away in his bag. Before we knew it we were able to have Brian for an overnight visit with us. We gave him a tour of his new home; the bedrooms, sound room and of course the teenage boys favorite the kitchen and pantry. What a life lesson Brian was already starting to teach me. He opened the pantry and just stared and said "I can't believe how much food you have." Wow! How many times had I stood in front of that same pantry and whined there was nothing to eat in it. How much we take for granted in this busy, materialistic world that emphasizes you must have the best of everything when so many would settle for anything. The fingerprints of God once again were all over this situation. While on a weekend visit Brian actually called me Mom. The child I was told would not do that for several years had not even moved into our home yet and was uttering the very words that were the sweetest sound on earth to me; "Mom". Oh, how we all anticipated and counted down until the day came for him to move into our home permanently. Then we would start our 90 day probationary period before the adoption would become legal. As the adoption time grew near the caseworker called with a request from the biological mother to meet us. The court-ordered visitation was continuing until the adoption was final. How awkward would this be? "Mom, meet Mom." I felt it best that we meet her. It would help us gain insight as to what Brian was dealing with. The day arrived and my anxiety was high. Why was I feeling anxious? I was the one doing a good deed. I prayed on the way to the meeting, "Lord please give me wisdom and prompt me to speak only when I should." I made one final request before my amen. "Please give me the opportunity to share you with this mother who is a victim of the cycle of abuse herself." As we walked into the room and were introduced my nerves began to subside. We had caseworkers and a therapist there to make sure things went smoothly. It was explained that we were adopting Brian and at that point the State would no longer be the mediator. Their Mother began to tell us how excited Brian was and what he had shared with her. She said Brian talked about going to church but stated that she was not sure if there was a God. Her mom calls her and tries to read her the Bible but she just hangs up. I could not sit silent after that statement I began to share how God brought me to Brian and predestined him to be a part of our family. I was hoping it would make an impact. I am not sure if she was touched by my witness or not, but I know that almost everyone there that day understood that this was 100% about God and his mercy. God's glory was certainly shining in the moment.

We picked Brian up and brought him home to a big banner that said "Welcome Home Brian" and he smiled, no laughed, at all the attention and celebrating that was taking place. Welcome home indeed!

The first several months were a rollercoaster with lots of loops and turns. The adjustment to the family and the family rules was not always received with open arms or minds. We were bringing such significant changes into his life. He was already a teen and the changes were overwhelming. I knew that no matter what, we needed to hold strong to the boundaries we had established. God clearly sets boundaries for us and wants us to do the same for our children. The feeling of being totally overwhelmed won out on some days but with the strength of Christ we held our ground and took one day at a time. After about three months of testing, bucking and releasing some stress the storm calmed. We felt so much more like a family. It is amazing how the negative spirit was overridden by the love of Christ which provided a light that could not be put out by the darkness that lives in Brian's eyes. God's hand was on so many aspects of this union. The child we thought was going to be absolutely impossible to handle was awarded "Camper of the Year" at the teen summer camp program he was attending. This was the same child that we were told by the former foster parents would not be able to remain in any such program and would be kicked out in less than a month. Praise God that he proved them all wrong!

The time came for our first visit to the psychiatrist to discuss the transition and to get an explanation of the medications the boys were currently on. This was not an experience that Brian looked forward to. He became very irritated at the prospect of the visit. I let him vent so I could get an idea of his issues with this doctor. The primary issue was that he felt as if they were not listening to him. The medication was making him tired and he could not even think. "They just want to give me drugs to make me sleepy all the time" he said angrily. I proceeded to explain that getting angry at the doctor was having the opposite effect he was looking for. "If you throw a fit and are out of control then the doctor is going to prescribe more meds not less. Let's try staying calm and me talking to the doctor to see what we can do to possibly reduce the medication so you are not so sleepy. I am not promising he will do that but we need to explain our case and listen to his reasons as to why you are taking so much medication." I said. "He won't listen." yelled Brian. "Can you at least let me try my way? What do you have to lose?" I countered. I could not tell him, but I had the same attitude about these doctors. All they wanted to do is pump kids full of medication instead of dealing with the underlying issues. So when the doctor came to the door to call us back I got in my strongest mother-bear-attack mode ready to go to battle for my son. As the doctor and I got acquainted it was revealed that he was a Christian. In discussing our family dynamic I found out that he had attended Palm Beach Atlantic University where my daughter was attending in the fall. He gave me the name of a Christian Church in the area and also told me he helped found an orphanage that my daughter could possibly work at. Since she was majoring in psychology that would be a perfect opportunity. It is amazing how God's shower of blessings comes in the moments you least expect them. I guess my stereotypical analysis of this doctor had been wrong. He listened to Brian's concerns about the medication he was taking and agreed that we would start reducing one of them with the goal of removing it totally if things went well. As we made our way back to the car, with a big smile Brian said "Thanks, Mom, for making him listen."

Were things perfect and in a heavenly bubble all the time? Absolutely not! We experienced the outbursts that we had read and been told about. The reaction and method by which we were able to deal with them required nothing short of Angels of God swooping down to help us and to protect us.

The school also suddenly seemed to have little angels in all the right places setting up methods to minimize the outbursts and keeping Brian in a public school with the least restrictive environment possible. The episodes we did have were dealt with accordingly. Brian was taught why some reactions were totally inappropriate. It was amazing to see the trust he began to build in us over this short period of time. He began to see that if the system was treating him unfairly then we would make sure it was changed to be fair. If he was handling things improperly then we would make sure that he changed things to make it respectful and fair. There was some resistance at first and he was not always happy with the consequences of his behavior. He was learning through the experiences and that was all we could hope for.

One more maneuver needed to happen to have me perfectly positioned to continue in the task God had given me. That morning doing my devotion I had this overwhelming feeling that something very upsetting was going to happen. When it did I needed to know that God was the one making the decision and he wanted me to be at peace about it. I briefly wondered about what was coming then shrugged it off and went to work. Then came the upsetting moment I had been warned about. I was called into my boss's office and told they were cutting back and I was on the chopping block. Wow! God surely wanted to ensure I experienced every aspect of life. This was definitely new to me. I had never been even slightly considered a candidate for firing or laying off. I was the foolishly dedicated team player who would do whatever needed to be done to get the task completed. 'How could this be happening to me?" I thought. After my head stopped reeling the tears began to well up in my eyes. I remembered that God had forewarned me of this moment and it had his blessing. This faith thing is never ending. God once again had chosen to make his presence known and had taken away my job two days before we were to adopt a teenager. I took a moment to drive around and clear my head before clearing out my desk. I am human after all and my pride had been deeply wounded. However, I had this inner voice telling me it was okay and to be at peace. It is hard to explain, but with the chaoius and confusion in my mind there was this peaceful feeling that everything was just as it was suppose to be. Psalm 46:10 says "Be still and know that I am God."

The next day I received a call from my former boss. This was the person I felt God had brought me to in the first place. Once again God's timing was so crucial. He had asked me to be patient and stay in my current job when I felt so uneasy. A year later when the timing was perfect He moved me exactly where I needed to be. My former boss told me that business was such he could justify another person and I was the perfect candidate. God is amazing! He made a loud statement by rocking my world right before the adoption so that true faith in trial could be witnessed. He then placed me in a respectful environment where I could earn the income I needed and still have the time I needed with my family. Thank you, God, for pushing us when we need a push and loving us enough to guide us to where we need to be to carry out our mission.

Friday was the big day. We were finally going to the courthouse for an adoption we had been striving for over the past four years. What a bundle of emotions that were going through my head. I was excited, scared, humbled and overwhelmed all at once. Talk about your head spinning! I would never have guessed when I started this journey that this would be the outcome. Here I was, by the grace of God, adopting a teenage son. Oh, I am so not worthy of this honored task of being a mother to this boy. "Oh God, how I want him to see you through me" was my prayer. To be able to give him hope and the opportunity he did not have before to accept you. And so this portion of my journey begins. Only God knows where things will go from here, but as I have shared with you thus far God has known exactly what he was doing.

It is amazing how you can see the fingerprints of God in your life if only you will take the time to look for them. From day one God had his hands on us and carefully executed His intended expansion of our family. He allowed circumstances in which we were able to stand up for Brian and have him believe in us and the goodness of God. It is so exciting when God uses us to be His hands and feet here on earth. It is not only a blessing to the person you are touching but a blessing in your life as well. That gives us the strength to tackle the next storm that comes our way.

There are so many lessons to be learned in life if only we will open our hearts and minds. We need to step outside the box that we have built around ourselves and experience all aspects of human existence. How unintentionally cold hearted we become when we box ourselves into our comfortable world and refuse to accept our true role in the world outside. We typically refuse to give up the comforts of our lives to give comfort to others in need. When Jesus walked on earth he did not only acquaint himself with the elite and well mannered or the rich and famous but also with the sinner, the poor, and the desperate needy. He gave them hope and performed miracles to change their current existence and make it better. The elite and well-to-do of that time shunned the less fortunate and literally secluded them from life. An example would be the leper who could not be touched because he was unclean. We read these stories in the Bible and think "how cruel, I would never do that to another human being." But in reality we do the exact same thing; sometimes worse. We turn our eyes away from the homeless, the poor and the abused. We may say, "That is unfortunate" but we do nothing to lend a hand to show them any hope or encouragement. Just like those lepers, we isolate ourselves from them and justify it by making it their problem and not ours. I am sure it breaks Jesus' heart to look down on the Christians of today and see how off base many of us are on our role here on earth. Christ came and lived the example for us to follow. He gave his life for the very people we will not even acknowledge.

He must be very disappointed and frustrated at our selfishness and closed minded thinking. Revelation 3: 15-16 states, "I know your deeds, that you are neither cold nor hot. I wish you were either one or the other! So because you are Lukewarm, neither hot nor cold, I am about to spit you out of my mouth."

I know one thing for sure, my mind is opened and I am making a very conscious attempt not to be judgmental. I have not lived the perfect life. Although I am not homeless, in prison, or neglecting my family it does not make my sins any less or my condition something earned. In God's eyes we are all sinners but by his grace can be redeemed. ALL OF US. I encourage you to start opening your heart and mind a little wider. Talk to Jesus daily and invite him into your life. The best thing I ever did was to ask God to allow me to see people through his eyes. What an amazing experience. It does not make your greatness and accomplishments any less. In fact, it makes you feel humbled that you have been blessed in your life. Others have been less fortunate and if you would just show them a Christ-like love they too could have the opportunity to find hope and joy and turn their lives around. Is everyone going to be saved? No, but we cannot justify our lack of trying with the excuse that they are hopeless. It is not our place to judge the heart of another person but to show them love so they can see the light to get out of the darkness. What if your judgment was wrong and you walked away with the remedy to cure their life? What a shame! I would much rather God have me down for trying even on the impossible ones and failing, than missing the ones that could have been saved by playing it safe. If you touch one person out of a hundred you attempt to touch you will still hear "Well done my good and faithful servant." Talk to God. Find out what gift he has given you and use it to its full potential. Bring a ray of light into this dark, dark world!

Philippians 1: 6

"Being confident of this, that he who began a good work in you will carry it on to completion until the day of Christ Jesus."